Workbook 2

GW00597326

My name is _____.

Mark Ormerod and Emma Mohamed

macmillan education

Macmillan Education
4 Crinan Street
London N1 9XW
A division of Springer Naure Limited

Companies and representatives throughout the world

ISBN 978 0 230 48905 9
Pack ISBN 978 1 380 00850 3

Text © Mark Ormerod and Emma Mohamed 2017
Design and illustration © Springer Naure Limited 2017

First published 2017

Original design by Wild Apple Design
Designed by Carolyn Gibson
Illustrated by Laura Avino, Alan Brown, Zara Buyukliiska, Tom Heard, Sarah Horne, Stu McLellan, Alex Orbe, Andrew Pagram, Jean Paul de Quay, Anthony Rule
Cover design by Bigtop Design Limited
Cover illustrations by Charlie Alder
Cover photographs by **123rf** wiml; **Alamy** Alex Segre; **Getty** EyeEm/Andrea Diotallevi, Alan Hopps, Pavlo_K; **Shutterstock** LiuSol, Christian Musat.
Recordings produced and arranged by James Richardson
Picture research by Julie-anne Wilce

Authors' acknowledgements
We would like to thank everyone at Macmillan Education, in both Spain and the UK, for their dedication and unfailing professionalism in the development and production of Heroes. Thanks also to the teachers who have given their time to read and pilot these materials. Their feedback has been truly invaluable. We'd like to thank the many teachers and students we have worked with over the years for the experience they have shared and the ideas they have inspired. And last but not least, we should like to thank our families for their support, patience and understanding. Special thanks from Mark to Carlos. Special thanks from Emma to Sue, Jose Luis, Danny and Nico.

The publishers would like to thank the following teachers:
Mónica Pérez Is, C.P. Eduardo Martínez Torner, Gijón (Asturias); Pilar Sánchez Vidal, CEIP Bellas Vistas, Alcorcón (Madrid); Inés Rosado Valdivia, Escola La Trama, Sabadell (Barcelona); Héctor Díaz, CEIP Severo Ochoa, Móstoles (Madrid); Adelaida Paunero, CEIP El Abrojo, Laguna del Duero (Valladolid); Verónica Ros Núñez, José Angel Funes Belmonte, Francesca Uceda Gómez, Mª José Conesa Ros and Rocío Moreno Parra, CEIP José Antonio, Fuente Álamo (Murcia); Bernabé González Mora, CEIP María Montessori, Móstoles (Madrid); Eva Alseda, Escola Gravi, Barcelona; Héctor Díaz, CEIP Severo Ochoa, Móstoles, (Madrid); Maite Meijide Ferreiro, CEIP Juan Antonio López Alcaraz, Puerto Lumbreras (Murcia); Mª Teresa Riaguas Torija, CEIP Gerardo Diego, Leganés (Madrid).

The authors and publishers would like to thank the following for permission to reproduce their photographs:
Alamy Blue Jean Images p29(7), Pearl Bucknall p5(8), Gareth Byrne p5(1), Opas Chotiphantawanon p26(1), David Cole p5(2), Cultura Creative (RF) p7(r), Cultura RM p20(6), Chuck Franklin p29(8), Stephen French p5(7), imageBROKER pp29,35(4),(cl), Image Source Salsa p29(1), Incamerastock p5(6), Juice Images p17(1), Robert Kerr p23(1), Lasse Kristensen p26(6), Luckyraccoon p38(3), MARKA p5(3), MITO images pp14,35(5),(tl), Mouse in the House 25(bed), Ben Nicholson p23(2), Sergey Novikov p31(c), OJO Images Ltd p29(2), ONOKY Photononstop p17(2), Phanie p7(cl), Eugene Sergeev p38(6), Alex Segre p5(5), Paul Springett 02 p23(6), Tetra Images p29(5), Viktoryia Yakubouskaya p26(3); **Corbis** Brownie Harris p31(cr), Ocean/Berit Myrekrok p20(1), Somos Images/ Steve Hix p7(cr); **Getty** ArtMarie p35(tr), Cristian Baitg p38(5), Blend Images/Jose Luis Pelaez Inc p35(cr), DAJ p31(cl), Danielle Donders p20(4), Evirgen p25(table), Hero Images p14(6), Inti St. Clair p17(3), Nino H. Photography p29(3), GEN UMEKITA p14(3), Dougal Waters p38(1); **Macmillan Publishers Ltd** 9904 p7(5), Corbis pp11,14(3)(5)(8)(lion)(penguin), (bl)(cl), Getty/Thinkstock p7(4), Getty/iStock/Thinkstock/ konstantin32 p7(3), JOHN FOXX IMAGES pp11,14(2),(cr), PHOTODISC P11(7)(giraffe); **Rex Shutterstock** Cultura p7(l); **Shutterstock** GUDKOV ANDREY p11(1)(crocodile), Natalia Barsukova p11(6)(flamingo), BestPhotoPlus p17(7), Bildagentur Zoonar GmbH p11(4)(ostrich), Andriy BONDAREV p23(5), Breadmaker p23(8), donatas1205 p25(shelves), geliatida p35(bl), Kaspars Grinvalds p38(4), g-stockstudio p7(6), David Hughes p23(7), julialine p17(6), luna4 p17(4), Felix Mizioznikov p14(1), Sergey Novikov p35(br), Alena Ozerova p17(5), Pavel L Photo and Video p20(3), Pix11 p26(5), Andrey Popov p29(6), Ppart p25(fridge), Michael puche p7(1), Rawpixel.com p25(car), Iriana Shiyan p23(4)(3), Ljupco Smokovski p26(4), Stocksolutions p25(bath), Sunny studio p17(8), Syda Productions p14(4), Thitisan p5(4), ThomsonD p38(2), Topimages p7(2), Stavchansky Yakov p14(2); **Thinkstock** istock/ Jani Bryson p20(2), e santis paolo p26(2), iStock/Photobuff p20(5).

Author photo (Mark Ormerod) by Antonio Blanco Otero
Author photo (Emma Mohamed) by Danny Garcia Mohamed

Printed and bound in Great Britain by Ashford Colour Press Ltd.

2021 2020 2019
10 9 8 7 6

Welcome back, Heroes!

1 Look, read and complete. Write about you.

HEROES FACT FILE

I'm Ruby.

I've got _a microphone_.

I want to sing.

HEROES FACT FILE

I'm _____.

I've _____.

I want to c _____.

HEROES FACT FILE

I'm _____.

I've _____.

I want to r _____.

HEROES FACT FILE

I'm _____.

I've _____.

I want to d _____.

HEROES FACT FILE

_____

_____

_____

Places

1 Listen and repeat. 1:14

2 Read, look and write.

> ~~funfair~~ theatre swimming pool school
> supermarket sports centre square safari park

 _funfair_

Pronunciation

3 Listen and say. Find the word that rhymes with *pool*. 1:15

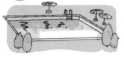 p o o l

Finished? Find four place words.

sportscentreschooltheatrefunfair

1 Look and write.

1 *sports centre*

2 _____

3 _____

4 _____

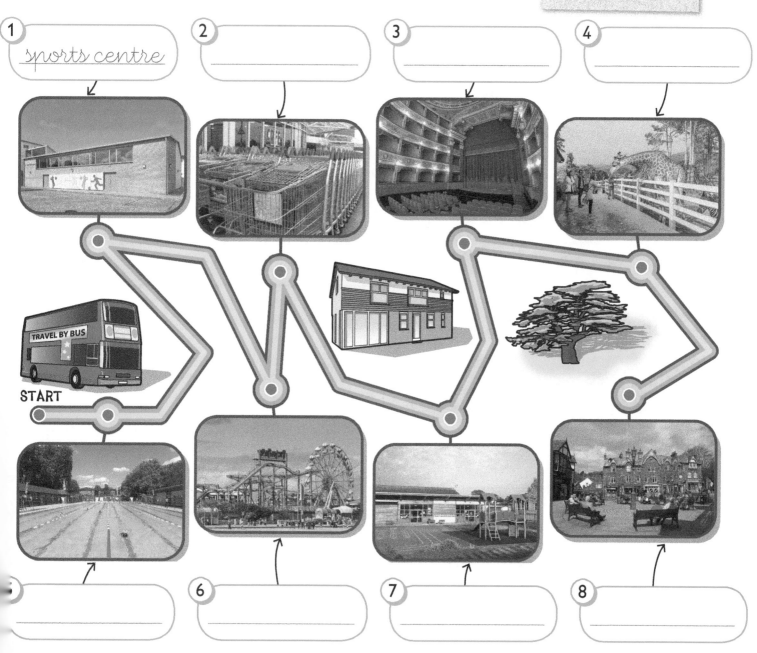

START

TRAVEL BY BUS

5 _____

6 _____

7 _____

8 _____

2 What's missing? Look and write.

The _____ and the _____ are missing.

Finished? Complete the words.

1 ___afari ___ark   2 ___unfair   3 ___upermarket

1 **Read and circle.**

Where's the sports centre / school?

It's here. It's next to the safari park / supermarket.

2 **Number and write.**

the funfair? ☐   Where's ☐

W_____ ⌐ _____ _____?

next to ☐   It's ☐   the theatre. ☐   It's here. ☐

It's _____. ⌐ _____ ⌐ _____ ⌐ _____

3 **Draw two places in your town. Write.**

Where's the _____?

It's _____

_____.

Finished? Ask a friend about their picture.

Say *Where's the …?*

1 Which four children think of other people? Circle.

2 Look and tick the things you do.

3 Read and think.

I'm a hero. I think of other people.

Finished? Draw a picture of the things you do.

1 Read, look and write.

~~car~~ bike tram boat bus train

1

2

3

_____car_____

4

5

6

_____ _____ _____

2 Listen. Follow and write. 1:30

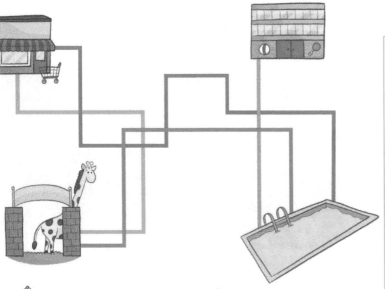

You can go to the safari park

by ___tram___ or by

_____.

You can go to the supermarket

by _____ or by

_____.

3 Write and say.

You can go to the _____.

Finished? Talk to a friend about places
and transport in your town.

1 Find and circle. ✏️

(funfair)theatreschoolsupermarketswimmingpoolsafariparksportscentresquare

2 Look and write. ✏️

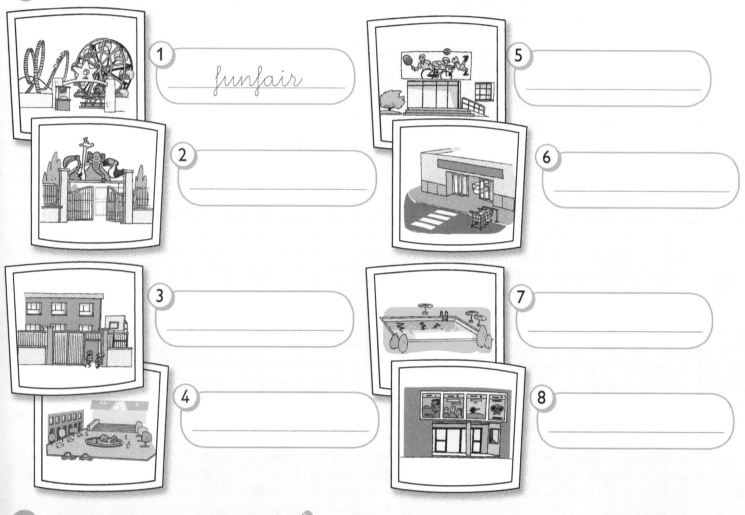

1. *funfair*
2. _____
3. _____
4. _____
5. _____
6. _____
7. _____
8. _____

3 Write the sentences. ✏️

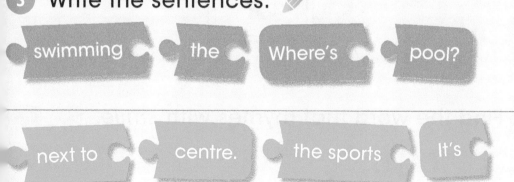

swimming | the | Where's | pool?

_____

next to | centre. | the sports | It's

_____

Mystery word

☐ ☐ ☐ ☐ ☐

Finished? Draw the mystery word. 📝

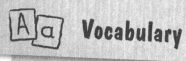
2 Wild animals

1 Listen and repeat. 1:34

2 Read, look and write. ✏️

Picture dictionary

> crocodile   penguin   giraffe   ostrich
> lion   flamingo   elephant   monkey

 *crocodile*

Pronunciation

3 Listen and say. Find the word that rhymes with *smile*. 1:35

 s   m   i   l   e

Finished? Find four wild animal words. ✏️

flamingoelephantostrichpenguin

1 Look and write. ✏️

1 _crocodile_

2 _____

3 _____

4 _____

Visit the ZOO

5 _____

6 _____

7 _____

8 _____

2 Look, match and write. ✏️

flamingo

giraffe

_____

1

2

3

4

5

6

penguin

crocodile

_____

Finished? Complete the words. ✏️

1 ___ro___odile   2 ___iraffe   3 ___la___ingo

11

1 **Read and circle.**

2 **Look and write.**

①
He _____ _____ swim.

②
It _____ _____ _____ fast.

③
_____ _____ _____ jump.

3 **Draw a friend. Write sentences.**

This is _____.

_____ can _____.

_____ can't _____.

Finished? Talk to your partner about your friend.
Say *This is … He / She …*

1 **Look and think. What's the problem?**

In your zoo, you've got three enclosures.
You've got five animals. Which three animals
can you put in the enclosures?
Which two animals can go free?

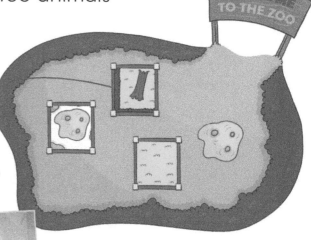

Think!
Which animals are dangerous?

2 **Now draw your solution. Draw the animals in the zoo.**

3 **Read and think.**

I'm a hero. I can solve problems.

Finished? Draw a picture of
you solving problems.

1 Look and write.

climb walk stand sit dive ~~fly~~

1

fly
_____

2

_____

3

_____

4

_____

5

_____

6

_____

2 Read and listen. Circle. 1:50

penguin

It can swim.	(True) / False
It can run fast.	True / False
It can fly.	True / False
It can sit.	True / False

monkey

It can swim.	True / (False)
It can dive.	True / False
It can stand on two legs.	True / False
It can walk and run.	True / False

3 Write about a lion.

_____
_____
_____
_____

Finished? Read the text to a friend.

1 Find and circle. Write.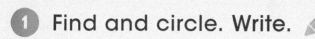

o	l	g	k	a	n	d	a	d	m
s	e	l	e	p	h	a	n	t	o
t	v	f	t	m	a	u	b	c	n
r	e	l	e	r	l	t	h	g	k
i	n	a	h	h	i	l	l	i	e
c	g	m	e	b	o	n	r	r	y
h	r	i	n	b	n	t	m	a	r
p	e	n	g	u	i	n	c	f	o
i	o	g	e	d	r	o	o	f	o
c	r	o	c	o	d	i	l	e	m

1 *lion*

2 _____

3 _____

4 _____

5 _____

6 _____

7 _____

8 _____

2 Write the sentences.

 fly.   penguin   A   can't

can   swim.   dive   It   and

Mystery word
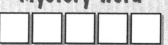

Finished? Draw the mystery word.

1 Listen and repeat. 1:54

2 Read, look and write.

> ~~beard~~   fair hair   curly hair   dark hair
> long hair   moustache   straight hair   short hair

 b_eard_

 l_____

 _____

 _____

 _____

 sh_____

 f_____

 s_____

Pronunciation

3 Listen and say. Find the word that rhymes with *chair*. 1:55

 c h a i r

Finished? Find four face words.

moustachecurlyhairbeardfairhair

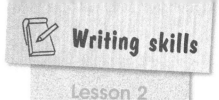
1 **Look and write.** ✏️

1
short hair

2 _____

3 _____

4 _____

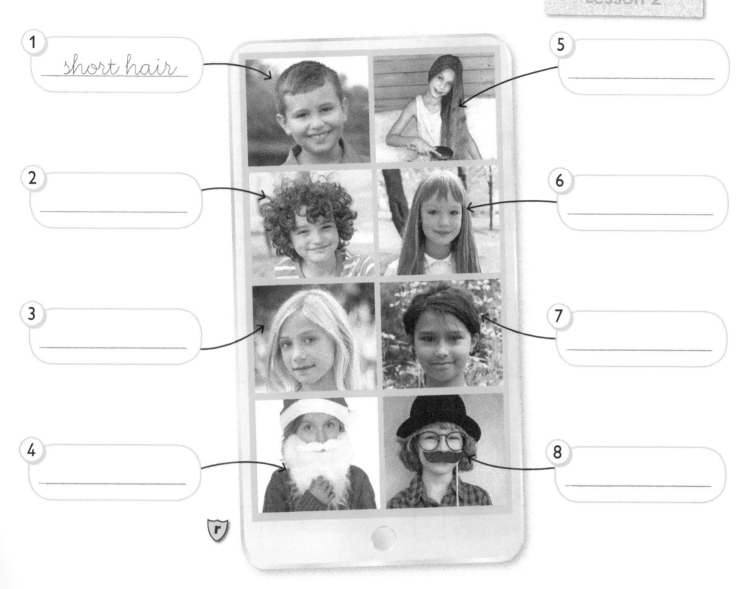

5 _____

6 _____

7 _____

8 _____

2 **What's next? Look and write.** ✏️

curly hair   dark hair   fair hair   curly hair   _____

Finished? Complete the words. ✏️

1 __urly __air   2 __ong __air   3 __eard

1 Read and circle.

Has he got long hair?

Yes, he has. /
No, he hasn't.

Has he got fair hair?

Yes, he has. /
No, he hasn't.

2 Number and write.

short hair? ☐   got ☐   Has she ☐

Has _____ _____ s_____ _____?

she hasn't. ☐   No, ☐   long hair. ☐   She's got ☐

No, _____ _____.   S_____ _____ I_____ _____.

3 Draw a friend. Write sentences.

_____ got _____.

_____ hasn't _____.

_____

Finished? Ask a friend about their picture.
Say *Has she / he got ...?*

1 Find the letters and numbers. Write.

m,_____   3,_____

2 Draw a face. Use letters from your name. Complete.

My name is _____.

3 Read and think.

I'm a hero. I can think creatively.

Finished? Draw a picture of a friend.
Use numbers and letters.

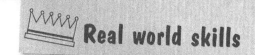
1 **Read, look and write.**

~~wig~~   mask   necklace   glasses   earrings   crown

1

wig

2

3

4

5

6

2 **Read and look. Write the number. Listen and check.** 2:15

1

2

3

4

She's got a necklace and a crown. She hasn't got a wig or earrings. ☐

She's got a crown and glasses. She hasn't got a necklace or earrings. ☐ 1

He's got _a crown_ . He hasn't got _____ . ☐

He's got _a mask_ . He hasn't got _____ . ☐

3 **Now look and complete. Read to a friend.**

Finished? Write about a friend.
Say _He's got … / She's got …_

1 Complete the words. ✏️

1 curly h_ai_r   4 sh__rt h____r

2 l_ng h___r   5 str____ght h___r   7 b____rd

3 m__st_ch__   6 d__rk h____r   8 f____r h____r

2 Look and write. ✏️

1 _curly hair_

2 _____

3 _____

4 _____

5 _____

6 _____

7 _____

8 _____

3 Write the sentences. ✏️

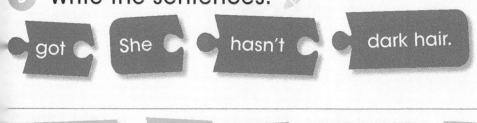

got   She   hasn't   dark hair.

_____

long hair   got   He's   a beard.   and

_____

Mystery word
☐☐☐☐☐

Finished? Draw the mystery word. 📝

21

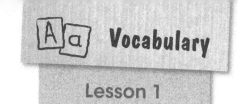
1 Listen and repeat. 2:19

2 Read, look and write.

attic   kitchen   living room   dining room

bedroom   garage   bathroom   hall

Picture dictionary

attic

Pronunciation

3 Listen and say. Find the word that rhymes with *ball*. 2:20

 b a l l

Finished? Find four home words.

hallbathroomkitchendiningroom

22

1 Look and write.

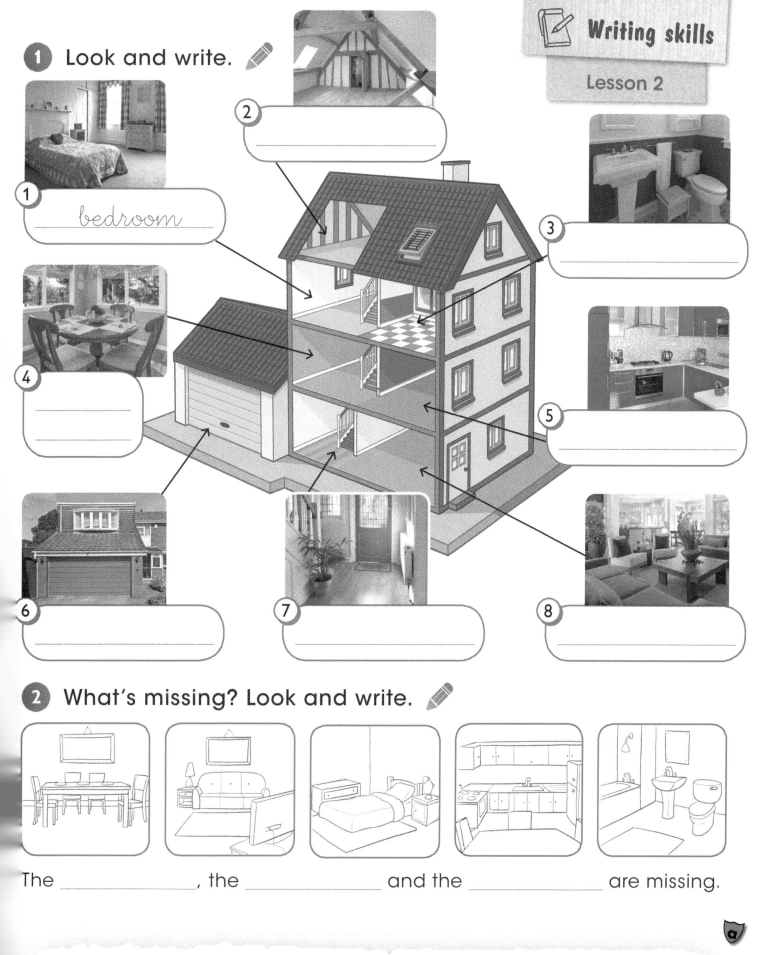

1 bedroom

2 _____

3 _____

4 _____

5 _____

6 _____

7 _____

8 _____

2 What's missing? Look and write.

The _____, the _____ and the _____ are missing.

Finished? Complete the words.

1 ___iving r___ ___m   2 a___ ___ic   3 ___ara___e

1 **Read and circle.** 🖉

There's / There isn't a monster in the kitchen.

There's / There isn't a monster in the dining room.

2 **Look and write.** 🖉

_____ a monster in the bathroom.

_____ a monster in the bedroom.

3 **Draw rooms and a monster. Write sentences.** 🖉

There _____

_____.

There _____

_____.

Finished? Show a friend your picture.

Say _There's … / There isn't …_

1 **Draw lines to match the objects and the rooms.**

books   dining room

car garage

table and chairs   bathroom

bed bedroom

fridge living room

bath kitchen

2 **Design a bedroom.**

3 **Read and think.**

I'm a hero. I make good decisions.

Finished? Write about your favourite room.

1 **Read, look and write.**

~~mirror~~   lamp   wardrobe   bed   sofa   bookcase

1

2

3

mirror

4

5

6

2 **Look and write the floor number. Listen and check.** 2:35

1 You can buy a bed on the ___fourth___ floor.

2 You can buy a mirror on the _____ floor.

3 You can buy a sofa on the _____ floor.

4 You can buy a table on the _____ floor and the _____ floor.

4ᵗʰ Floor
bedroom department

3ʳᵈ Floor
bathroom department

2ⁿᵈ Floor
living room department

1ˢᵗ Floor
kitchen department

Ground Floor
garden department

3 **Complete. Ask and answer.**

Where can I buy a _____?

On the _____.

Finished? Say _You can buy a ..._
on the ...

1 Find and circle. Write.

g	l	g	k	a	n	d	a	d	f
d	i	n	i	n	g	r	o	o	m
r	v	o	t	m	a	u	b	c	b
n	i	e	c	r	r	t	h	e	a
d	n	w	h	h	a	l	l	m	t
a	g	u	e	b	g	n	r	c	h
t	r	n	n	b	e	t	m	n	r
t	o	c	o	b	b	d	c	a	o
i	o	b	e	d	r	o	o	m	o
c	m	e	m	a	n	d	r	y	m

1 *bedroom*

2 _____

3 _____

4 _____

5 _____

6 _____

7 _____

8 _____

2 Write the sentences.

the garage. | in | There's | car | a

_____

isn't | the kitchen. | a sofa | There | in

_____

Mystery word

☐ ☐ ☐ ☐ ☐

Finished?
Draw the mystery word.

Routines

Picture dictionary

1 Listen and repeat. 2:39

2 Read, look and write.

go rollerblading   learn French   walk the dog   play tennis

watch a film   go shopping   see friends   go swimming

go rollerblading

Pronunciation

 g

3 Listen and say. Find the word that rhymes with *frog*. 2:40

f r o g

Finished? Find four routine words.

seefriendsgorollerbladingplaytennisgoswimming

1 Look and write. ✏️

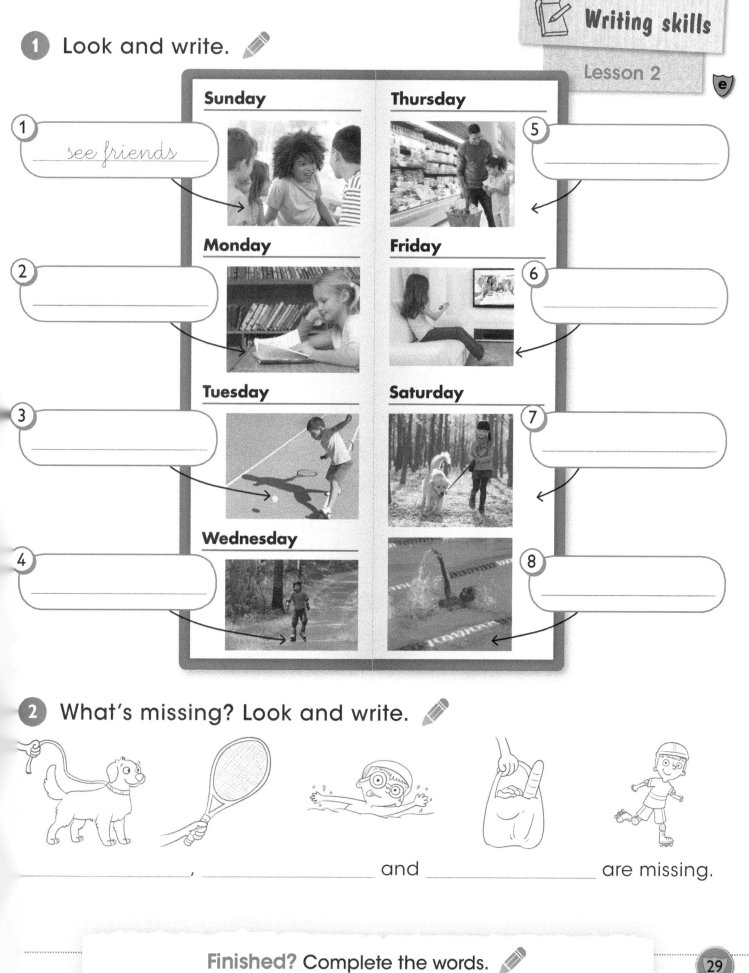

Sunday

1 *see friends*

Monday

2 _____

Tuesday

3 _____

Wednesday

4 _____

Thursday

5 _____

Friday

6 _____

Saturday

7 _____

8 _____

2 What's missing? Look and write. ✏️

_____ , _____ and _____ are missing.

Finished? Complete the words. ✏️

1 l____rn Fr__nch   2 ___atch a f__lm   3 s_____ frie____s

1 Read and circle. 🖉

Do you go swimming on Thursday?

Yes, I do. / No, I don't.

THURSDAY

Do you go rollerblading on Saturday?

Yes, I do. / No, I don't.

SATURDAY

2 Number and write sentences. 🖉

on Saturday? □　you □　Do □　go shopping □

Do ___ g_____ ?

I don't. □　I □　on Saturday. □　No, □　go rollerblading □

N__, _____ .　I _____ _____ .

3 Draw an activity. Write sentences. 👤 🖉

Saturday	Sunday

On _____, I _____ .

_____

Finished? Show a friend your picture.
Ask your friend *Do you ... on ...?* 💬

1 Who's working together? Circle.

2 Look and match. Tick the things you do together.

play games   work   clean the classroom

3 Read and think.

I'm a hero. I work well with other people.

Finished? Draw a picture of how you work well with other people.

1 Read, look and write.

~~wake up~~   have breakfast   have dinner   go to bed

do homework   do gymnastics

wake up

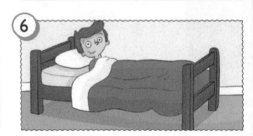

2 Read and listen. Circle the differences. 2:55

Dear Friend,

My name is Lisa. I like gymnastics. Every day,
I get up and I go to the funfair. I do gymnastics for
three hours. Then I have dinner and go to school.
After school, I go rollerblading for one hour and I do
my homework. Then I have lunch and I go to bed.
Write to me. Tell me about you.

Anna

3 Now write about you.

Before school, I _____

After school, I _____

Finished? Talk about your routine.
Say *After school, ...*

1 **Read and match.**

watch	shopping
go	a film
learn	rollerblading
go	French

see	swimming
play	tennis
walk	friends
go	the dog

2 **Look and write.**

1  *watch a film*

2  _____

3 BONJOUR! _____

4 _____

5 _____

6 _____

7 _____

8 _____

3 **Write the sentences.**

Saturday? | on | you | Do | go shopping

_____

on | Friday. | I | the dog | walk

_____

 **Mystery word**

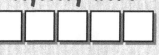

Finished?
Draw the mystery word.

6 Holidays

Picture dictionary

1 Listen and repeat. 🔊 3:04 💬

2 Read, look and write. ✏️

making a sandcastle   painting a T-shirt   playing badminton   playing volleyball
~~fishing~~   making a bracelet   snorkelling   painting a picture

fishing

Pronunciation

3 Listen and say. Find the word that rhymes with *skirt*. 🔊 3:05 💬

s   k   i   r   t

Finished? Find three holiday words. ✏️

snorkellingplayingvolleyballfishing

34

1 Look and write. ✏️

Have a great summer!

1 _painting a picture_

2 _____

3 _____

4 _____

5 _____

6 _____

7 _____

2 Look, match and write. ✏️

playing badminton

fishing

1

2

3

4

5

6

painting a picture

playing volleyball

_____

_____

Finished? Complete the words. ✏️

1 __ishing   2 pla__ing __adminton   3 snorke__ling

1 Read and circle.

Are you painting a picture?

No, I'm not. / Yes, I am.

Are you playing badminton?

Yes, I am. / No, I'm not.

2 Number and write.

a ☐   making ☐   I'm ☐   sandcastle. ☐

_____

a picture? ☐   you ☐   Are ☐   painting ☐

_____

3 Draw yourself. Write a sentence.

I'm _____

_____

_____

Finished? Show a friend your picture.

Ask *Are you …?*

1 Colour yellow for a summer holiday and blue for a winter holiday.

2 Organise the bags. Draw.

summer

winter

3 Read and think.

I'm a hero. I'm very organised.

Finished? Think about the things you need for a summer holiday. Write.

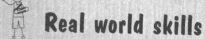
1 **Read, look and write.**

lifeguard   sun cream   sun hat   sandals   flag   water

lifeguard

2 **Listen and number.** 3:19

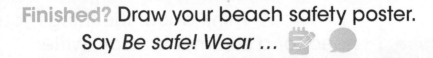

Finished? Draw your beach safety poster.
Say *Be safe! Wear ...*

1 Look and write.

1 <u>making a sandcastle</u>

2 _____

3 _____

4 _____

5 _____

6 _____

7 _____

8 _____

2 Write the sentences.

at · Are you · playing · the beach? · volleyball

_____

snorkelling · I'm · the sea. · in

_____

Mystery word

☐ ☐ ☐ ☐ ☐

Finished?
Draw the mystery word.

Units 1 and 2 review

Listening

1 Listen and tick.   3:20

1 What's Leila's favourite wild animal?   **2** Which bird can fly?

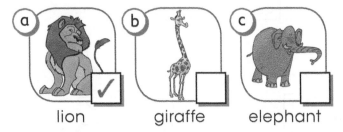

lion   giraffe   elephant

ostrich   flamingo   penguin

3 What's next to Leila's school?   **4** How does Leila get to school?

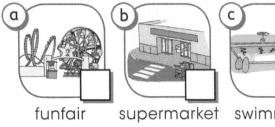 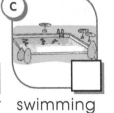

funfair   supermarket   swimming pool

 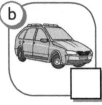 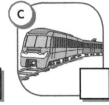

by bus   by car   by train

2 Listen to Tom. Write a one-word answer.   3:21

Me

1 Can you swim?   Yes   _____

2 Has your school got a swimming pool?   _____   _____

3 Do you like safari parks?   _____   _____

4 What's your favourite type of bird?   _____   _____

5 How do you get to school?   _____   _____

3 Read and answer the questions for you.

CYL **Cambridge Young Learners exam practice: Starters**

4 Find and circle.

g b u s k k r p t r a i n n m p f l a m i n g o z x q f u n f a i r j x p s c h o o l d l i o n

5 Look and write.

1 _bus_

2 _____

3  _____

4  _____

5 _____

6  _____

6 Read and look. Write *Yes* or *No*.

1 The crocodile is green.
   Yes

2 The giraffe is next to the elephant.
   _____

3 The flamingo can't stand on one leg.
   _____

4 A penguin is in the water.
   _____

7 Talk about the picture.

There's a …

Where's Supercat?

Supercat is on / next to the bike.

Finished? How many can you find in the picture?

people   animals   types of transport

41

Exam practice

Listening

1 **Listen and tick.** 3:22

1 Who's Tom's dad?

2 Who's Tom's grandma?

3 What's Tom's favourite room?

4 What has Tom got in his bedroom?

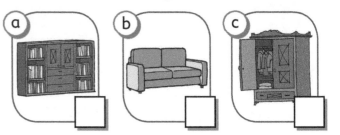

2 **Listen to Emma. Write a one-word answer.** 3:23

 Me

1 Have you got dark hair? No _____

2 Is your hair long or short? _____ _____

3 What colour is your bathroom? _____ _____

4 Have you got a computer in your bedroom? _____ _____

5 At home, where do you eat? _____ _____

3 **Read and answer the questions for you.**

 Cambridge Young Learners exam practice: **Starters**

4 Circle the different word.

1 wardrobe (wig) bed
3 long curly necklace

2 crown wig kitchen
4 hall dining room moustache

5 Look and write.

garage

rgaega

ksma

rabed

irormr

6 Read and look. Write *Yes* or *No*.

1 There's a mirror on the wall.

Yes

2 There's a lamp next to the bed.

3 There isn't a wardrobe.

4 There's a book on the floor.

Where's Supercat?

Supercat is next to / under the bed.

7 Talk about the picture.

There's a ...

Finished? How many can you find in the picture?

clothes books animals toys

Exam practice

Listening

1 Listen and draw lines. 3:24

| Jack | Donna | Rita | David | Bobby | Jackie |

2 Listen to Zack. Write a one-word answer. 3:25

  Me

1 What's your favourite day of the week?   Sunday   _____

2 What do you do after school?   _____   _____

3 Do you go to the beach in the summer?   _____   _____

4 Can you play badminton?   _____   _____

5 What colour is your favourite T-shirt?   _____   _____

3 Read and answer the questions for you.

 Cambridge Young Learners exam practice: **Starters**

4 Look and write.

1
water

wetra

3
_____

entins

2
_____

errollingblad

4
_____

nadlass

5 Read and complete.

~~friends~~   swimming   breakfast   dog

1   On Saturday, I see my _*friends*_ and I walk the _____ .

2   Before school, I go _____ and I have _____ .

6 Read and look. Write one-word answers.

1 What day is it? *Saturday*

2 What colour is the car? _____

3 How many people
   can you see? _____

4 Are they in the
   bedroom? _____

7 Talk about the picture.

There's a …

Where's Supercat?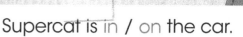

Supercat is in / on the car.

Finished? How many objects in the picture can you name?

Remember the story.

A rocket ride

1 **Look, find and tick.** ✎

 ✓

2 **Remember and order. Match.** ✎

(in the museum)   (on the moon)   (in the park)

3 **Read and write.** ✎

(**My story words**   museum   park   ~~plane~~   rocket)

1 The ___museum___ is next to the _____.

2 The ___plane___ is next to the _____.

4 **Think and colour.** ✎

I think the story is scary   interesting   sad

47

The story of Kookaburra

1 **Look, find and tick.**

  ✓

2 **Look, read and match.**

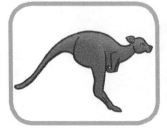   

It can climb.   It can jump.   It can laugh.   It can sing.

3 **Read and write.**

My story words: kangaroo   koala   sing   ~~laugh~~

1 It's a kookaburra. It can _____*laugh*_____ .

2 It's a _____. It can jump.

3 It's a _____. It can't _____.

4 **Think and colour.**

I think the story is   happy   sad    scary

Where's Grandma?

1 Look, find and tick.

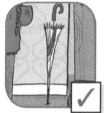 ✓

2 Remember and order. Match.

Look, it's only a mask!

It's Grandma.
I think she's a wolf.

I'm not different.

3 Read and write.

My story words   ~~grey hair~~   sharp teeth   umbrella   raincoat

1 She's got ___grey hair___ and _____.

2 She's got a red and white _____ and
a _____.

4 Think and colour.

I think the story is   😒 boring   😊 funny   😮 scary

TREASURE AT THE LIGHTHOUSE

1 Look, find and tick.

2 Remember and order. Match.

in the garden   in the kitchen   in the study

3 Read and write.

My story words   ~~cupboard~~   chest   garden   study

1 There's a ___cupboard___ in the _____.

2 There's a _____ in the _____.

4 Think and colour.

I think the story is boring   sad   exciting

A monster weekend

1 **Look, find and tick.**

 ✓ ☐ 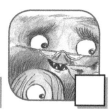 ☐  ☐  ☐  ☐

2 **Look, read and match.**

I go running on Saturday.

We work hard at school.

Charlie and Monty Monster are good friends.

Let's walk the dog now.

3 **Read and write.**

My story words   work hard   relax   stay with   ~~go home~~

 **1** I _go home_ _____.

 **2** At school, I _____.

 **3** After school, I _____ Monty.

 **4** At Monty's house, I can _____.

4 **Think and colour.**

I think the story is  boring    funny   scary

The magic shell

1 Look, find and tick.

 ✓ 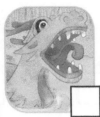 ☐  ☐  ☐  ☐ 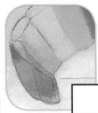 ☐

2 Look, read and match.

What's your wish, Alex?

I want to go on the river.

I want my friends here again.

I want to fly.

3 Read and write.

My story words   collecting shells   rowing a boat   lifejacket   kite

 1 Look! I'm *collecting shells* _____.

 2 Look! I'm flying. I've got a _____.

 3 Look! I've got a _____. I'm _____.

4 Think and colour.

I think the story is  happy   scary   exciting

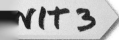 

1 Charlie and Monty
Monster are good friends.

Come on, Charlie.
Time to go home.

OK, Mum. Bye, Monty.

8 At Charlie's house

You want to go to bed and
you want to go to school?

Yes, Mum. I want to go
to school so I can relax.

4 It's Saturday.

I'm Big-Foot Fred.

I'm One-Eye Elsie.

Let's walk the dog
now, Charlie.

5 Three hours later

I'm Six-Leg Susie. I go
running on Saturday.

Come on. Let's all
run home together.